ESSENTIAL KEYBOARD REPERTOIRE

75 EARLY/LATE INTERMEDIATE SELECTIONS

TO DEVELOP TECHNIQUE AND MUSICIANSHIP

Baroque to Modern

SELECTED AND EDITED BY
MAURICE HINSON

Second Edition
Copyright © MCMXCV by Alfred Music
All rights reserved. Produced in USA.

Cover design: Martha Widmann   Art direction: Ted Engelbart

Cover art: *A Schubert Evening in a Viennese Home*, 1897
by Julius Schmid (1854–1935)
Oil on canvas
Erich Lessing/Archiv für Kunst und Geschichte, London

ESSENTIAL KEYBOARD REPERTOIRE
TO DEVELOP TECHNIQUE AND MUSICIANSHIP

Selected and Edited by Maurice Hinson

CONTENTS

This edition is dedicated to
Dr. Timothy Woolsey
with admiration and
appreciation.

Maurice Hinson

Foreword

Piano literature contains wonderful repertoire for the intermediate student that focuses on developing specific technical and musical mastery. The piano literature is so extensive that it is frequently difficult for the teacher and student to locate some of the attractive musical pieces to develop technique and repertoire. *Essential Keyboard Repertoire to Develop Technique and Musicianship* is designed to assist with this common problem. Some of this literature is well known, while other selections may not be so familiar.

The purpose of this collection is to provide "essential keyboard repertoire" for developing the technical and musical growth of the intermediate-level pianist. The editor has carefully selected interesting music, and even though a number of the pieces are entitled "Etude," none were written to develop only technique. Each piece is an effective and expressive work that presents a specific facet of keyboard technique while developing musicianship. Each piece is an etude and each etude is a piece.

J. S. Bach composed his six partitas, *Italian Concerto, Overture in the French Style*, the "Goldberg" Variations and other works, under the title *Clavier-Übung*, meaning "Keyboard Exercises." Domenico Scarlatti labeled his first 30 keyboard sonatas *Essercizi per gravicembalo* (Exercises for Harpsichord). The word *Essercizi* should be understood in much the same sense as the etudes of Chopin; these works are not mere technical exercises but rather artistic essays that explore specific devices such as scales, arpeggios and broken chord figuration.

Musical etude pieces are included from the 18th, 19th and 20th centuries. The areas of technique and musicianship emphasized in this collection are: broken chords, crossing hands, double notes and chords, finger action, legato, loose wrist, perfect coordination, repeated notes, staccato and two- and three-note slurs. Each area is considered vital by the editor in building technique and musicianship. Pedal is necessary in many of these pieces and can be considered a technical skill that any musical pianist must master.

The Intermediate-Level Student

The intermediate level is a crucial period in the development of a pianist. It encompasses the period of time when a student is nearing completion of beginning method books but is not quite ready to move on to advanced works by the great composers.

Individual students reach this level at different rates, depending on their ability, age and previous experience. To facilitate easy use, this collection is divided into three levels: *early intermediate* (EI), *intermediate* (I) and *late intermediate* (LI). These levels are identified by the letters EI, I and LI attached to each musical etude piece listed in the section "Contents Listed by Categories."

Students at the *early-intermediate* level should be able to play the scales of C, G, D and F major, plus D and A minor. These students should also be able to perform musically the pieces in J. S. Bach's *Anna Magdalena Notebook* or similar pieces of equivalent difficulty. Material for this level should approximate *Level 3* of *Alfred's Basic Piano Library*.

Students at the *intermediate* level should be able to play the scales of C, G, D, F and B-flat major, plus D, A, E and G minor. At this level, students should be able to play some of the easier dances in J. S. Bach's *Notebook for W. F. Bach*, easier dances by Beethoven and other pieces of equivalent difficulty. The repertoire and minimum technical requirements for this level approximate *Level 4* of *Alfred's Basic Piano Library*.

Students at the *late-intermediate* level should be able to play the scales of C, G, D, A, E, F, B-flat, E-flat and A-flat major, plus A, D, E, G, B, C, F-sharp and C-sharp minor. Appropriate repertoire for this level should approximate *Levels 5–6* of *Alfred's Basic Piano Library* or more difficult works such as selected *Two-Part Inventions* of J. S. Bach and *Sonatinas* of Kuhlau.

The editor hopes that you will find much pleasure in playing these attractive musical-etude-pieces, and will thereby develop solid technical and musical growth as well as a new appreciation for this repertoire.

What Is Technique?

Technique is the means by which musical ideas are expressed; technique must be perfected so that musical ideas may be made clear. In the intense desire to perfect technique, the object of making music is often overlooked, and the piano student may forget that he/she is trying to achieve musical performance. A great artist is not great simply because he/she has a wide range of tone color, fine finger action, a velvety touch, or free and strong arm movements, but because he/she has musical ideas to express and the technique to express them. Without musical ideas, the most perfect technical equipment leaves the listener unmoved, except to excite the same kind of admiration seen in a fine acrobatic performance. The spirit of the music is found in the musical idea, and the spirit cannot be expressed without the proper technique. When seen from this point of view, technique and musical performance are vitally intertwined.

What Is Musicianship?

The way that a pianist handles the musical subtleties of a piece depends mainly on sensitivity and an innate instinct for aesthetic correctness. These and other related qualities fall under the umbrella term "musicianship." A strong sensitivity to the emotions of music—one's ability to perceive and react to its stimulus—is generally a good indication of musicianship. All of the following are considered part of musicianship: tempo, accent, variation of tone (including coloring and shading), articulation, individuality, careful variation from rigid rules and the poetic vision of the interpreter. All of these come into play when a pianist tries to reproduce in sound the inspired conceptions of the great composers. All nuances cannot be indicated. The pianist well grounded in musicianship understands the signs on the page and their complete significance in relation to the other implied and printed indications. "That a genius like Chopin did not indicate everything accurately is quite explainable," wrote Moritz Rosenthal. "He flew, where we merely limp after."[1]

Patient Study

Patience is required to perfect musicianship and a reliable technique. Great lessons in patience can be learned from people like Thomas Edison, who sometimes spent 17 or 18 hours without interruption in his laboratory, working intensely on experiments. It is not the amount of time spent, but the *kind* of practicing one does that is important. Some students, in a hurry, try to learn a piece by repeatedly playing it over, while the more serious student learns by a careful, slow, analytical process that goes to the foundation of its technical and musical requirements.

The great French piano teacher Isidor Philipp (1863–1958) said: "Practice slowly, without any stiffness, with intelligence and reflection. Practice with a perfectly free arm and supple hands. Practice with different rhythms, different movements, different attacks and different nuances. Practice with patience—and always with patience."[2]

Editing

Great care has been given to the layout and engraving of this music. Each piece appears in its original form; notes have not been added or removed, unless stated otherwise. When articulation, notes, pedal, dynamics or interpretive indications have been added by the editor, they are always identified in footnotes or parenthetically. Either more or less pedal may be used than is indicated in some pieces, depending on room acoustics, the sound of the instrument and the personality of the player. Fingerings are based on modern teaching principles and are editorial. Measures are numbered for easy reference. The indications **f–mp** (or other dynamics) mean that the section is to be played forte the first time and mezzo piano on the repeat.

1 Mary Venable. *The Interpretation of Piano Music.* Boston: Oliver Ditson Co., 1913: 6.

2 Isidor Philipp. *Complete School of Technic for the Piano.* Bryn Mawr, Pennsylvania: Theodore Presser Co., 1908: 3.

Contents Listed by Categories

Broken Chords: Broken chords include Alberti bass figures as well as arpeggio passage-work. Evenness in broken-chord playing is vital for a musical performance, especially when transferred between hands. In Alberti basses, fingers should remain in contact with the keys to control dynamics most effectively. Broken chords frequently contain melodies that must be projected in performance.

Crossing Hands: This musical and technical device has been used by composers for centuries to provide an extension of range. Keep the hand crossing over close to the other hand (low) with an economy of motion. The use of the forearm is involved in each crossing.

Double Notes and Chords: Notes must be played exactly together and at the same volume unless one is to be brought out for melodic, accent or other purposes. Careful listening is required for musical sonority.

Finger Action: Evenness and precision are required for effective finger action. A finger lifted too high may cause strained conditions and a hard tone; a finger lifted too low will not give a sufficient clearness. Curved and well-raised fingers at a medium height should provide the crisp finger work required for a musical performance of all of these pieces.

Legato: Legato is like walking. When one walks, the weight of the body is transferred from one foot to another for each step. In playing a smooth, connected musical legato, the weight of the hand and arm must go easily from one finger to the next.

Loose Wrist: A baby placed in front of a keyboard pats the keys with outstretched fingers and natural limp wrists. This loose wrist is what one must have to produce a musical tone quality. The principle of relaxation plays a large part in developing loose, supple and yielding wrists, as well as the idea of playing easily, with no stiffness or strain.

Perfect Coordination: Metric and rhythmic precision are essential to artistic performance. The figures ♫ ♩ or ♪♩ ♪

are difficult for students to play. Count the four 16ths or four 32ds so that the fourth subdivision is exactly correct and quieter than the long note. Be sure all notes of chords sound exactly together.

Repeated Notes: A change of finger on repeated notes has been the rule for many years. This frequently results in unevenness due to the varying lengths of the fingers. It is sometimes easier and more musical sounding to use the same finger on repeated notes. Try both ways in the following compositions and use the one that produces the best musical sound, even if it differs from the editorial fingerings.

Staccato: There are many degrees of staccato: lightly detached notes, short, sharp, robust or dry staccato. Either fingers or wrist (or both) action is required in all the pieces. Stay close to the keys and use slower action for the lightly detached notes. Finger staccato should not be played by simply moving the fingers quickly up and down, but by slightly drawing in the fingertip. Wrist staccato should be executed with the hand, the wrist being free and supple and fingers rounded.

Two- and Three-Note Slurs: For the two-note slur, simply say "down up" while playing the two notes, connecting the first to the second. Make sure the second note is softer than the first one for a good musical effect. Think of floating off the second note. For three-note slurs, say "down roll up" to describe the physical activity of the hand. Think of floating off the third note.

Contents
Listed by
Composer

Contents
Listed by
Title

Contents Listed by Level

English Ballet

Johann C. F. Fischer
(ca. 1665–1746)

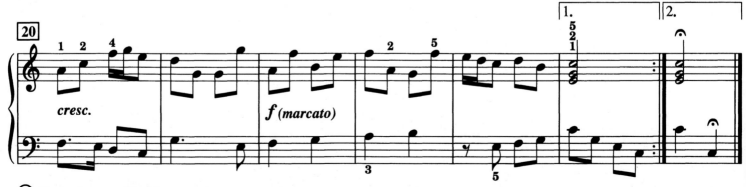

(a) Dynamics are editorial.

Allegro in A Minor

Domenico Zipoli
(1688–1726)

(a) Dynamics and articulation are editorial.

Etude in B-flat Major

Johann Christian Bach
(1735–1782)

ⓐ Dynamics and articulation are editorial.

Etude in F Major

Johann Christian Bach
(1735–1782)

ⓐ Dynamics and articulation are editorial.

Allegro in B-flat Major

Wolfgang Amadeus Mozart (1756–1791)

K. 3

ⓐ Dynamics are editorial.

Scherzo in F Major

Johann Friedrich Reichardt
(1752–1814)

(Allegro vivo ♩ = ca. 126)

ⓐ Dynamics are editorial.

Etude in E Minor

Johann Wilhelm Hässler
(1747–1822)

ⓐ Dynamics and articulation are editorial.

Lullaby

César Franck
(1822–1890)

(a) Dynamics and articulation are editorial.

Etude in E Major

Cornelius Gurlitt (1820–1901)
Op. 82, No. 98

ⓐ Pedal indications are editorial.

Prelude in C Major

Theodor Kirchner
(1823–1903)

ⓐ Pedal indications are editorial.

Kite Settled on the Branch

Béla Bartók (1881–1945)
Sz. 42:II/2

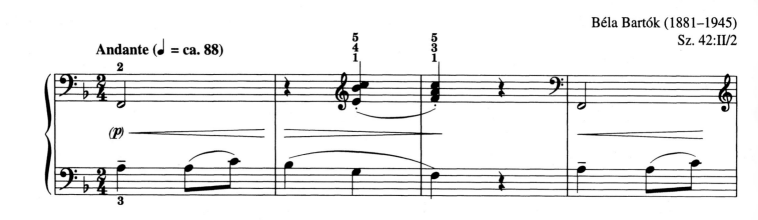

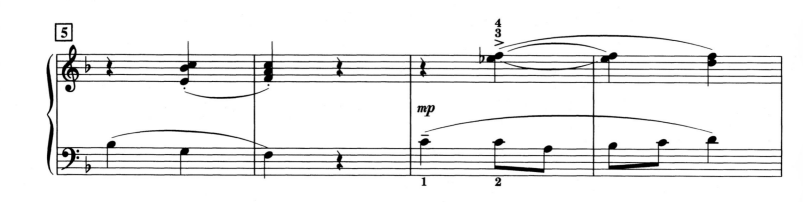

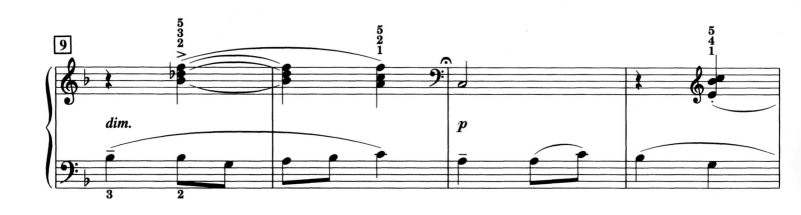

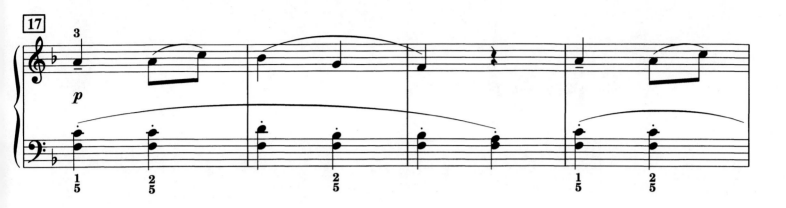

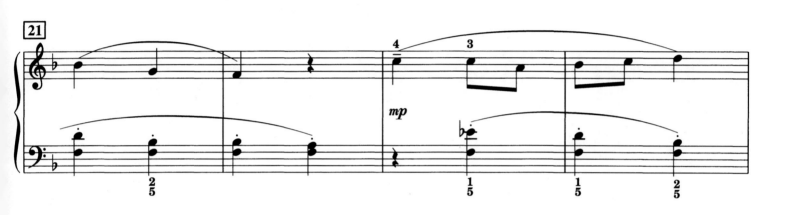

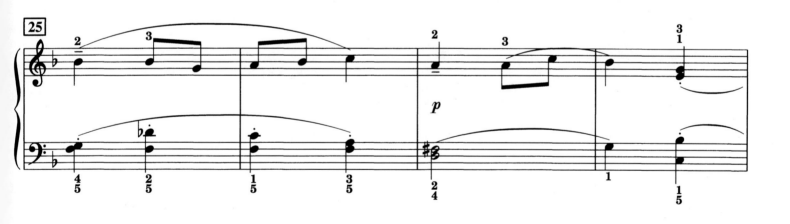

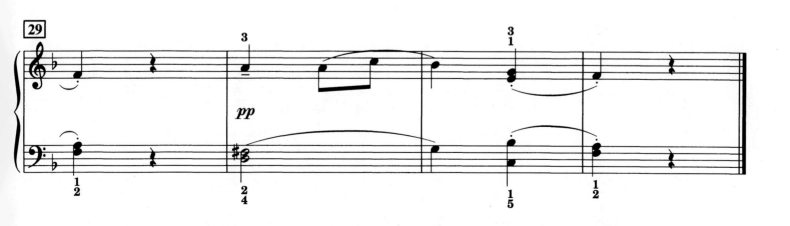

Strolling

Alexander Gretchaninoff
(1864–1956)

A Sad Tale

Dmitri Kabalevsky (1904–1987)
Op. 27, No. 3

A Brisk Game

Dmitri Kabalevsky (1904–1987)
Op. 14, No. 1

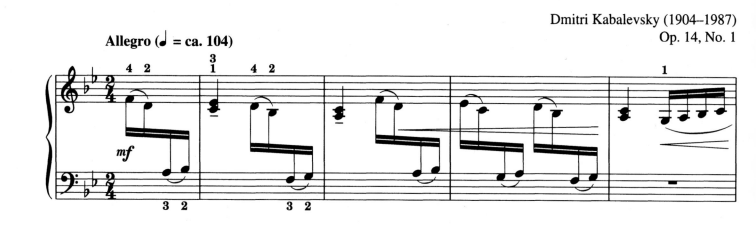

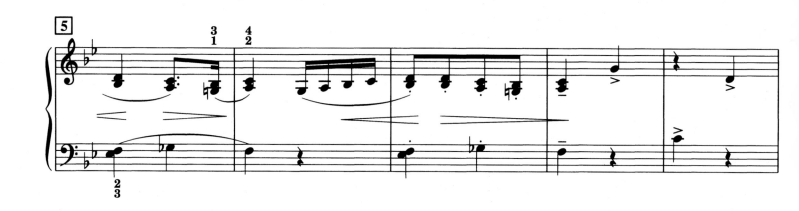

Country Dance

Dmitri Kabalevsky (1904–1987)
Op. 39, No. 17

The Juggler

Dmitri Kabalevsky (1904–1987)
Op. 89, No. 21

Sonata in C Major

Domenico Scarlatti (1685–1757)

K. 95

ⓐ Dynamics and articulation are editorial.

Pastoral

Domenico Scarlatti (1685–1757)
K. 415

ⓐ Dynamics and articulation are editorial.

Sonata in G Major

Domenico Scarlatti (1685–1757)
K. 431

ⓐ Dynamics and articulation are editorial.

Bourrée in D Minor

George Frideric Handel
(1685–1759)

(a) Dynamics and articulation are editorial.

Bourrée

from *Suite in F Major*

Johann Sebastian Bach (1685–1750)
BWV 820:5

ⓐ Dynamics and articulation are editorial.

Praeludium in D Minor

Johann Sebastian Bach (1685–1750)

BWV 851

(Andante ♩ = ca. 56)

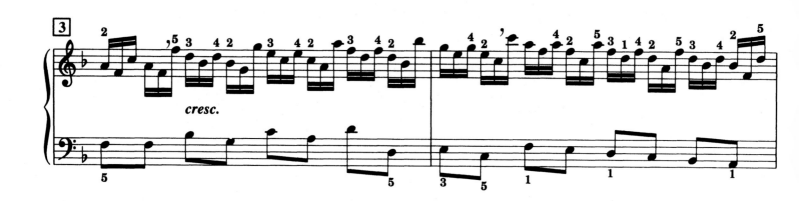

ⓐ Dynamics are editorial.

ⓑ Commas (') are editorial and indicate short silences.

This early 15-measure version of the Praeludium in D Minor was found in the *Clavier-Büchlein vor Wilhelm Friedemann Bach.* J. S. Bach later expanded this prelude to 26 measures in the *Well-Tempered Clavier, Book 1.*

ⓒ **This chord may be arpeggiated at the performer's discretion.**

Toccata in E-flat Major

Johann Ludwig Krebs
(1713–1780)

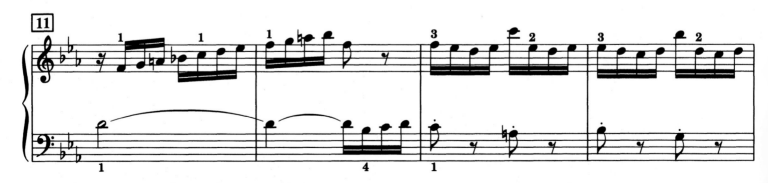

ⓐ Dynamics and articulation are editorial.

March in D Major

Leopold Mozart
(1719–1787)

ⓐ Dynamics and articulation are editorial.

A Hunting Jig

Leopold Mozart
(1719–1787)

ⓐ Dynamics, articulation and pedal indications are editorial.

Presto in C Minor

Carl Philipp Emanuel Bach (1714–1788)
Wq. 114:3

ⓐ Dynamics are editorial.

Andante con Moto

Francesco Pasquale Ricci
(1732–1817)

ⓐ Dynamics, articulation and pedal indications are editorial.

Minuet in B-flat Major

Johann Christian Bach
(1735–1782)

(Allegretto ♩ = ca. 104)

ⓐ Dynamics and articulation are editorial.

Con Portamento

Johann Christian Bach
(1735–1782)

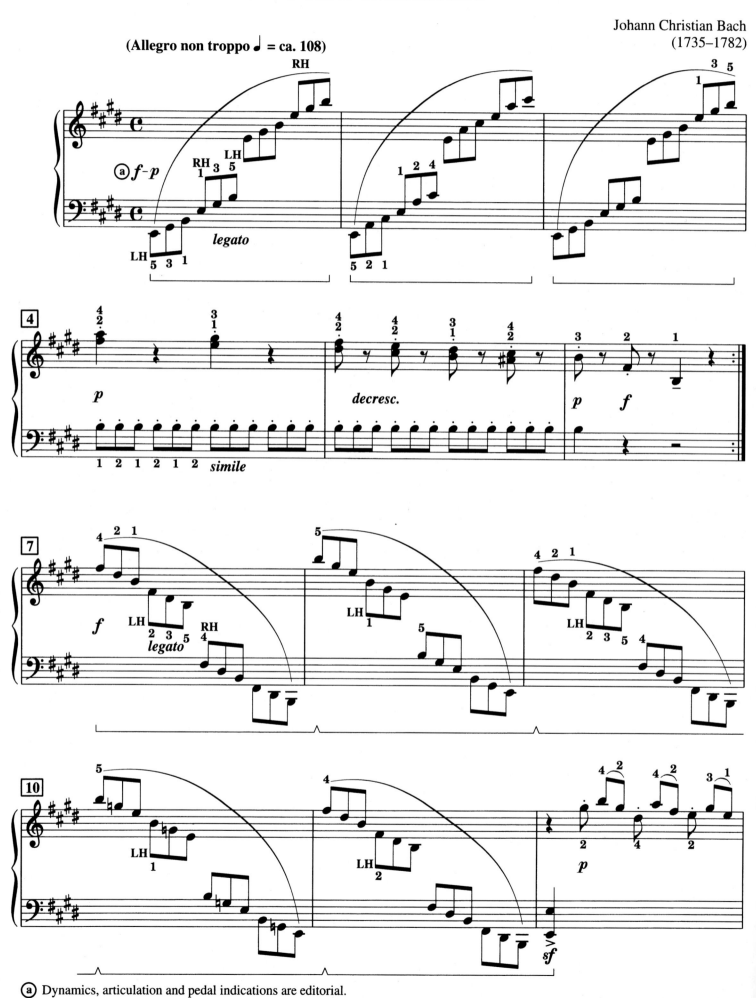

(a) Dynamics, articulation and pedal indications are editorial.

ⓑ The original piece ended here. The last five measures have been added by this editor.

Allegro Scherzando in F Major

Franz Joseph Haydn (1732–1809)
Hob. III:75/4

ⓐ Dynamics are editorial.

Minuet in D Major

James Hook
(1746–1827)

ⓐ Dynamics and articulation are editorial.

Viennese Waltz

Ludwig van Beethoven (1770–1827)
WoO 17, No. 3

ⓐ Dynamics and pedal indications are editorial.

Waltz in E-flat Major

Muzio Clementi
(1752–1832)

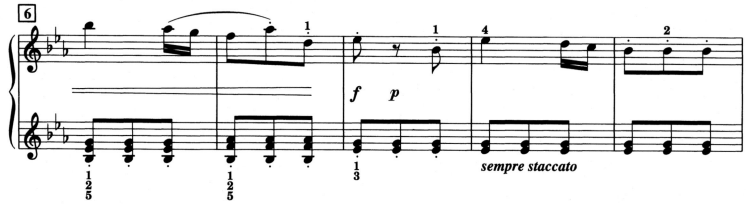

Study in D Major

Daniel Gottlob Türk
(1756–1813)

(a) Dynamics are editorial.

Andantino

Jan Ladislav Dussek
(1760–1812)

a Dymamics are editorial.

Capriccietto

Johann Nepomuk Hummel
(1778–1837)

Allegretto giusto (♩ = ca. 100)

ⓐ Dynamics and pedal indications are editorial.

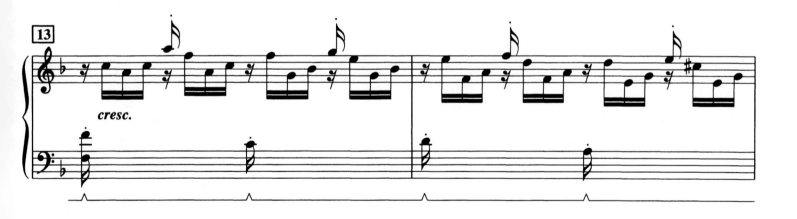

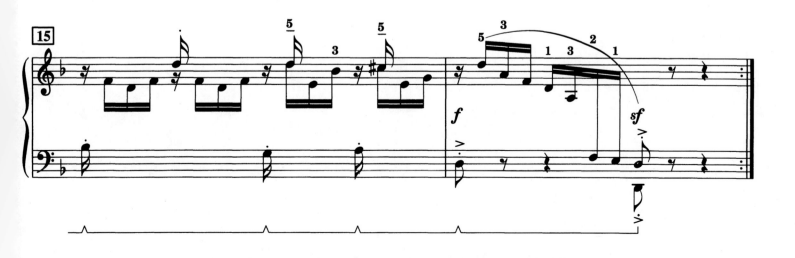

Capriccio

Johann Nepomuk Hummel
(1778–1837)

ⓐ Dynamics and pedal indications are editorial.

Etude in A Minor

Johann Nepomuk Hummel
(1778–1837)

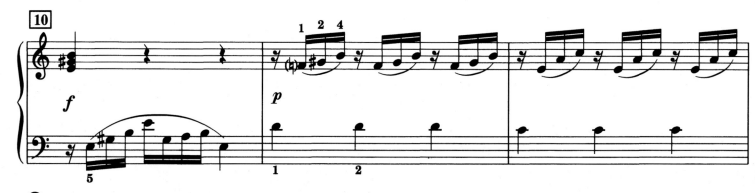

ⓐ Dynamics, articulation and pedal indications are editorial.

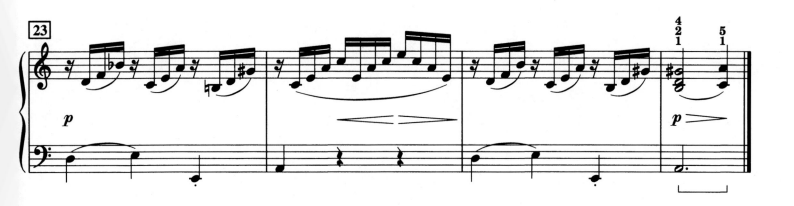

Agitato

Johann Friedrich Burgmüller (1806–1874)
Op. 109, No. 8

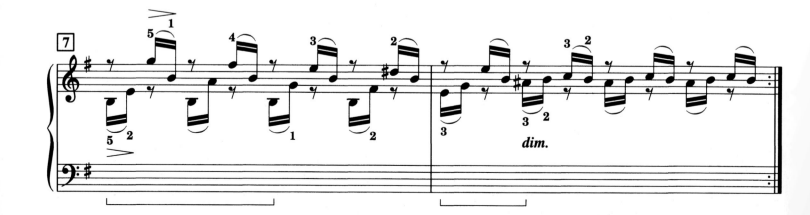

Bourrée in A Major

Frédéric Chopin (1810–1849)
BI 160b:2

(a) Pedal indications are editorial. (b) [musical notation] (c) The final A in the second ending is editorial.

Prelude in F Major

Theodor Kirchner
(1823–1903)

ⓐ Dynamics are editorial.

Arietta

Edvard Grieg (1843–1907)
Op. 12, No. 1

Poco andante e sostenuto (♩ = ca. 54)

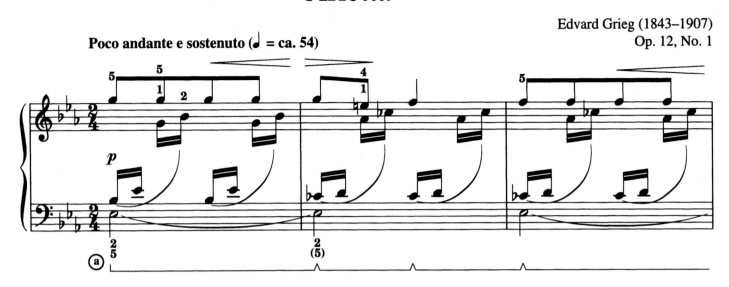

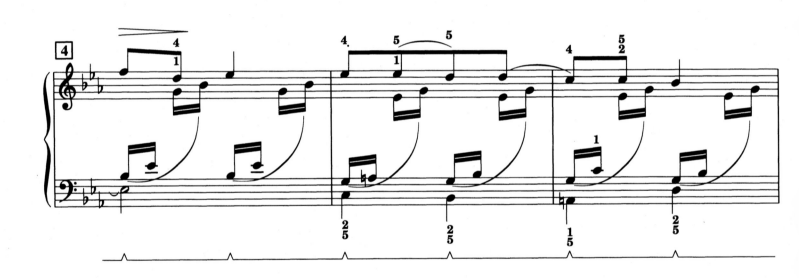

ⓐ Pedal indications are editorial.

Duetto

Souvenir of Beethoven

Stephen Heller (1813–1888)
Op. 47, No. 15

Scherzino

Stephen Heller (1813–1888)
Op. 119, No. 3

Con moto scherzando (♩. = ca. 76)

ⓐ Dynamics are editorial.

Mazurka

Peter Ilyich Tchaikovsky (1840–1893)
Op. 39, No. 10

Allegro non troppo (♩ = ca. 126)

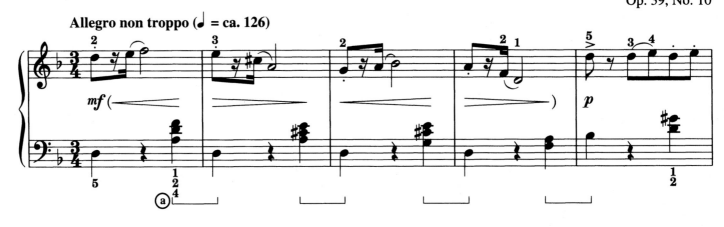

ⓐ Pedal indications are editorial.

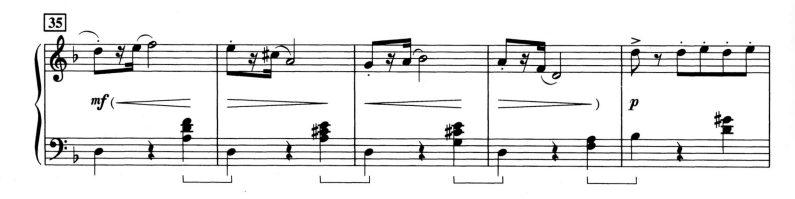

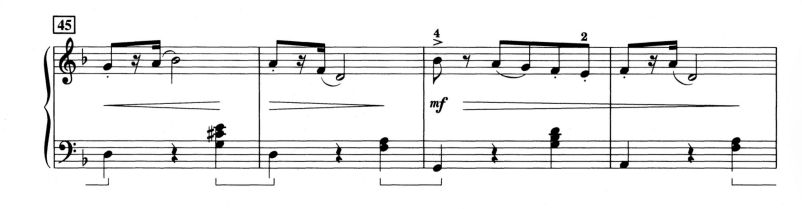

Playing Horse Games

Peter Ilyich Tchaikovsky (1840–1893)
Op. 39, No. 3

82

Secrets

Amy Beach (1867–1944)
Op. 25, No. 5

(a) Pedal indications are editorial.

Allegro

Béla Bartók (1881–1945)
Sz. 42:38

Folk Dance

Béla Bartók (1881–1945)
Sz. 42:6

89

Folk Song

Cyril Scott
(1879–1970)

ⓐ Pedal indications are editorial.

A Happy Story

Dmitri Shostakovich (1906–1975)
Op. 69, No. 4

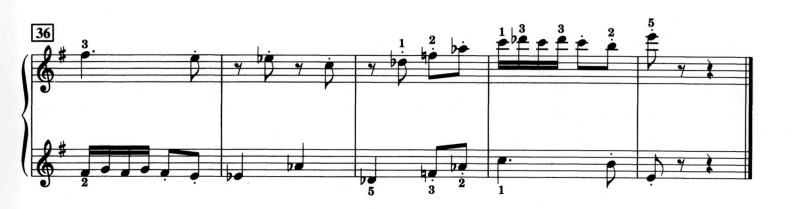

Country Dance

(Lively and nimble ♩ = ca. 152)

Dmitri Shostakovich
(1906–1975)

Etude in A Minor

Dmitri Kabalevsky (1904–1987)
Op. 27, No. 8

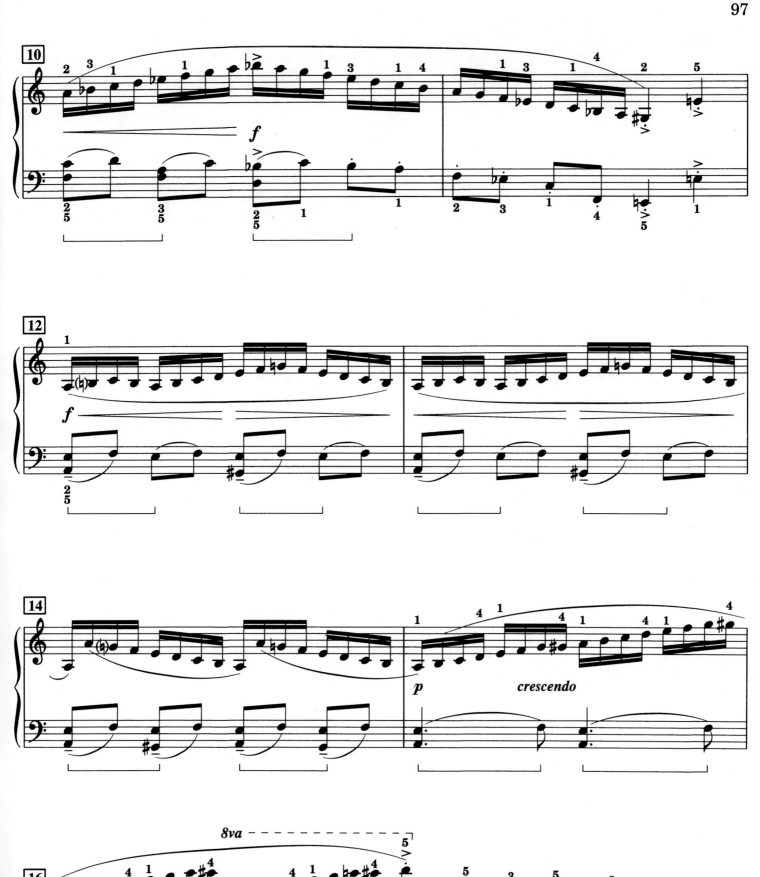

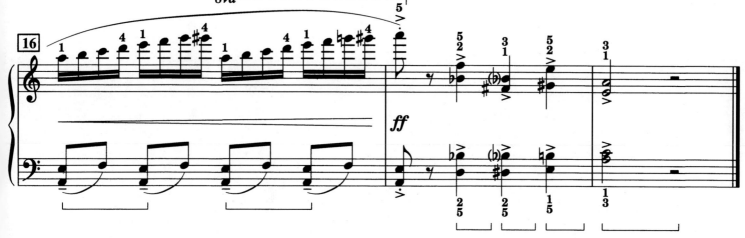

Gentle Waltz

Dmitri Kabalevsky (1904–1987)
Op. 39, No. 23

Andante tranquillo ($\quad$ = ca. 108)

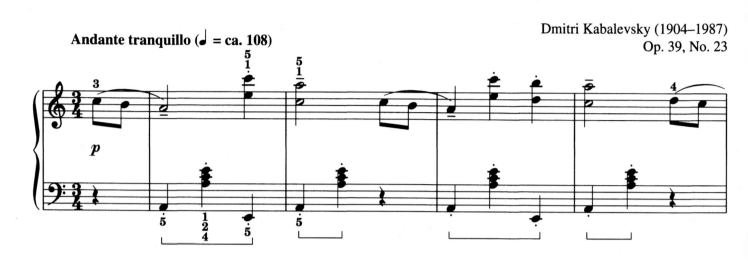

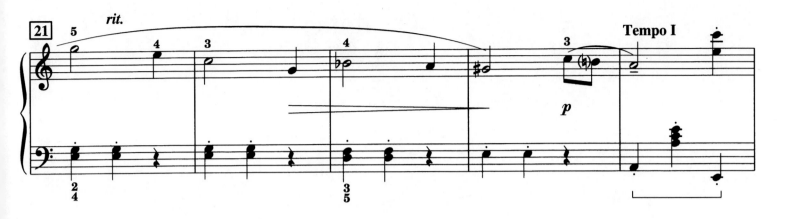

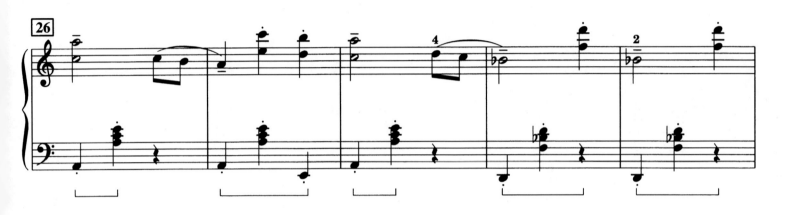

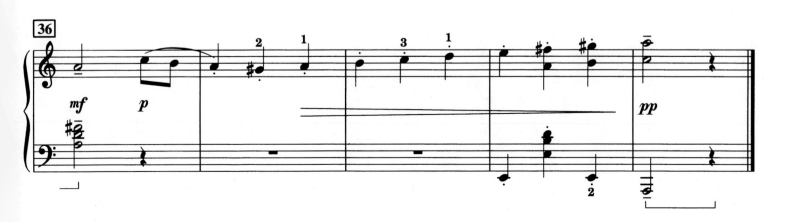

The Drummer

Dmitri Kabalevsky (1904–1987)
Op. 14, No. 2

Allegro moderato, tempo di marcia (♩ = ca. 88)

ⓐ Pedal indications are editorial.

Sonata in G Major

Domenico Scarlatti (1685–1757)
K. 391

ⓐ Dynamics, articulation and pedal indications are editorial.

Toccata in F Minor

Carl Philipp Emanuel Bach (1714–1788)
Wq. 63:6

(a) Original title.
(b) Dynamics and pedal indications are editorial.

Etude in G Major

Johann Wilhelm Hässler
(1747–1822)

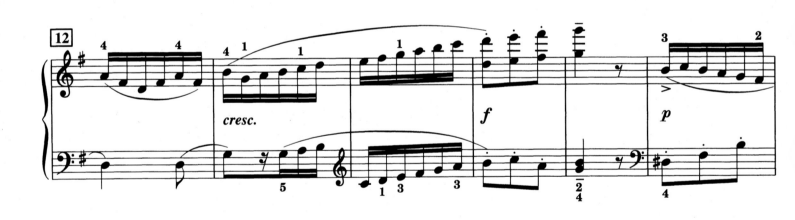

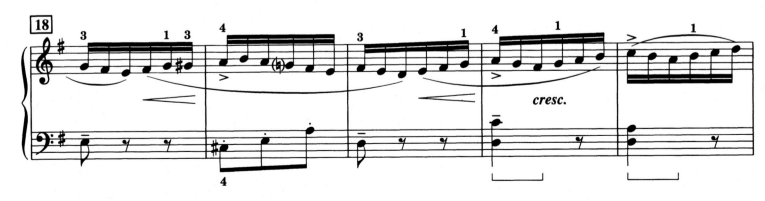

(a) Dynamics and pedal indications are editorial.

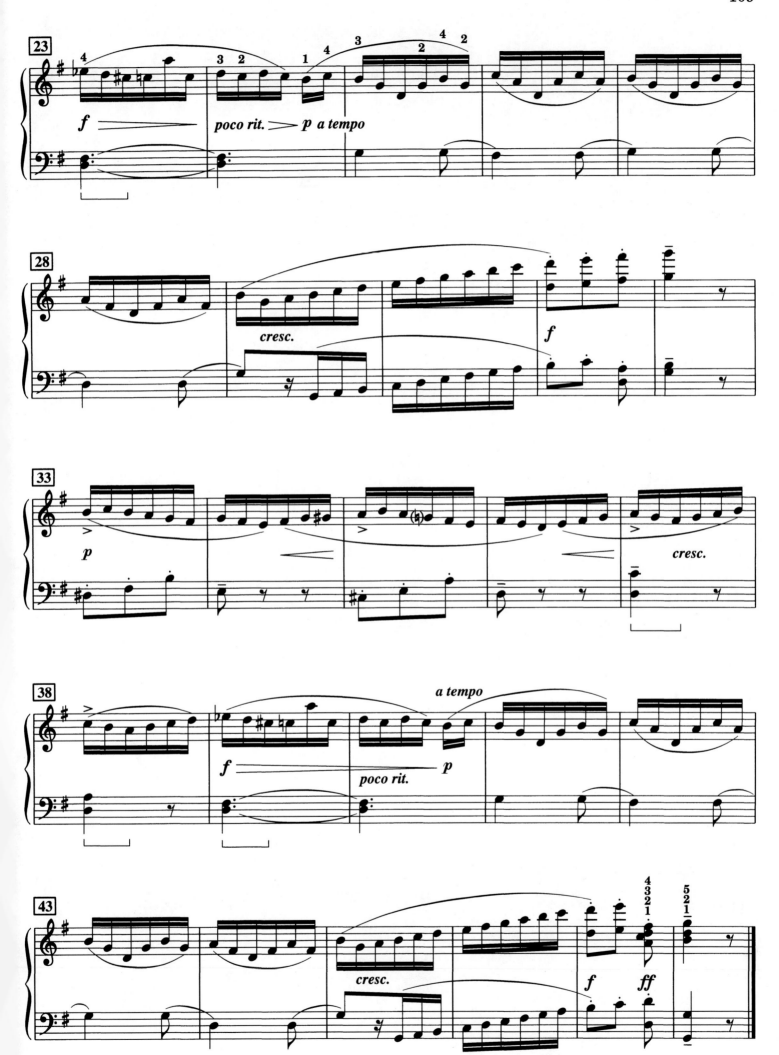

For Gertrude

(Waltz)

Ludwig van Beethoven (1770–1827)
WoO 16

(a) Dynamics, articulation and pedal indications are editorial.

Menuetto
from *Sonata in D Major*

Ludwig van Beethoven (1770–1827)
Op. 10, No. 3

ⓐ Pedal indications are editorial.

Waltz in G Major

Muzio Clementi (1752–1832)
Op. 38, No. 1

D.C. al Fine

Hungarian Melody

Franz Schubert (1797–1828)
D. 817

(a) Pedal indications are editorial.

Allegro Agitato

Carl Czerny (1791–1857)
Op. 821, No. 88

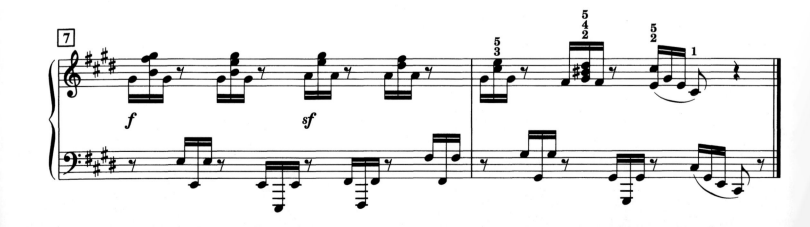

Sostenuto

Frédéric Chopin (1810–1849)
BI 133

ⓐ Pedal indications are editorial.

Important Event

Robert Schumann (1810–1856)
Op. 15, No. 6

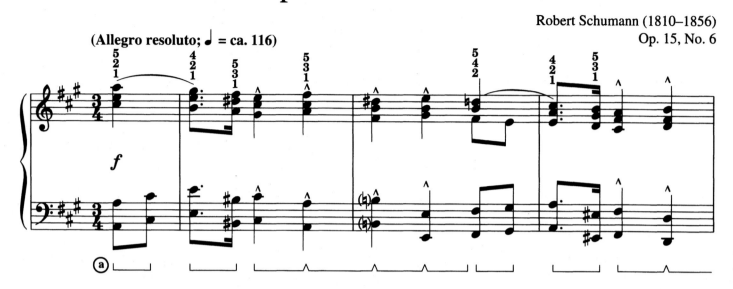

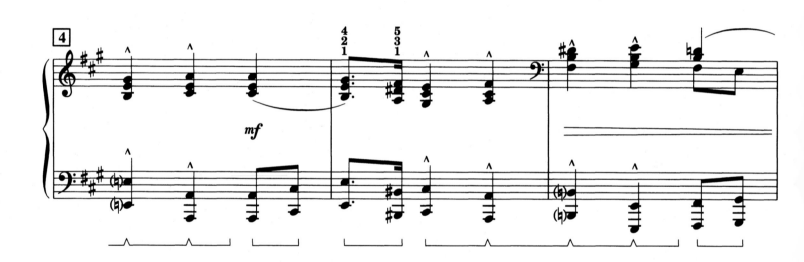

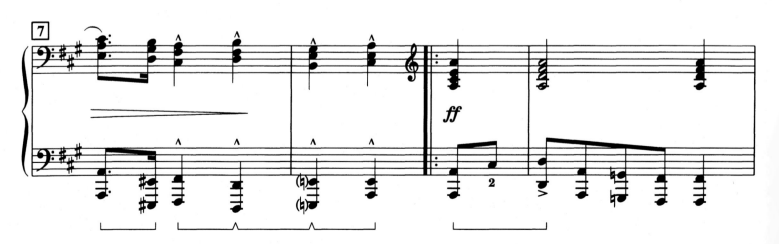

ⓐ Pedal indications are editorial.

Piano Piece in A-flat Major No. 2

Franz Liszt (1811–1886)

S. 189a

(a) Pedal indications are editorial.

Capricious Etude

Theodor Kirchner
(1823–1903)

Prelude in E Minor

Allegretto giusto ($\bullet$. = ca. 69)

Theodor Kirchner
(1823–1903)

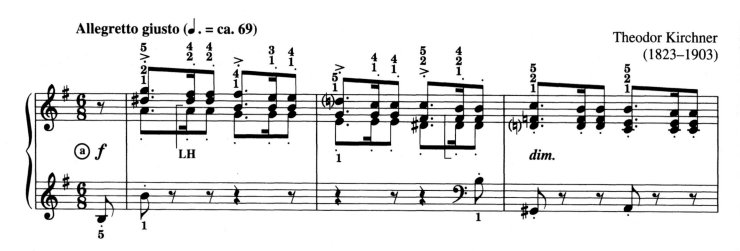

ⓐ Dynamics are editorial.

Waltz in F Major

Stephen Heller
(1813–1888)

ⓐ Pedal indications are editorial.

Waltz in A Major

Johannes Brahms (1833–1897)
Op. 39, No. 15

(a) Simplified version by Brahms.   (b) Pedal indications are editorial.

Spanish Marionettes

Allegretto scherzando (♩. = ca. 72)

César Cui
(1835–1918)

ⓐ *pp*

ⓐ Dynamics are editorial.

Prelude in D Minor

Arthur Foote (1853–1937)
Op. 53, No. 2

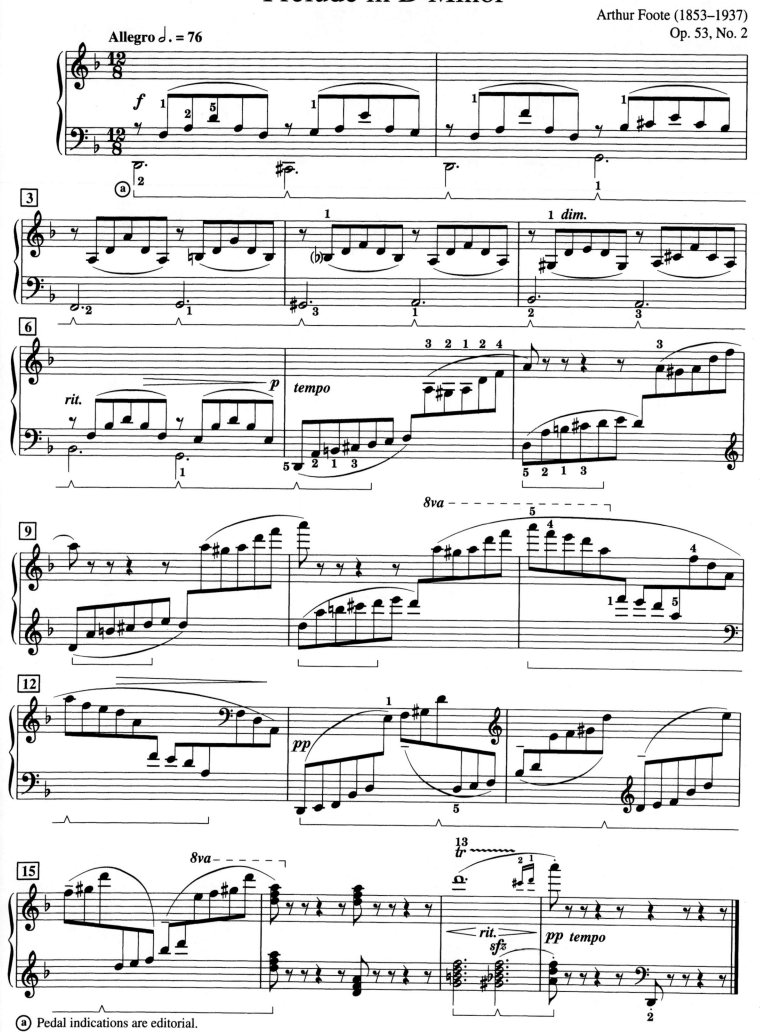

ⓐ Pedal indications are editorial.

Prelude

Maurice Ravel
(1875–1937)

(Rather slowly and very expressive [rhythmically free] ♩ = 60 approximately)
Assez lent et très expressif (d'un rythme libre) ♩ = 60 environ

ⓐ Pedal indications are editorial.

Village Dance

Béla Bartók (1881–1945)
Sz. 42:32

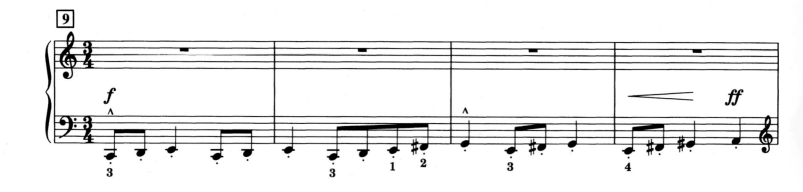

Etude

Aram Khachaturian
(1903–1978)

ⓐ Pedal indications are editorial. Fingerings, except those in parentheses, are the composer's.

144